MW01388207

Modern Disciples 365

Kevin Raines

Order this book online at www.trafford.com
or email orders@trafford.com

Most Trafford titles are also available at major online book retailers.

Print information available on the last page.

ISBN: 978-1-6987-0375-6 (sc)
ISBN: 978-1-6987-0376-3 (e)

Library of Congress Control Number: 2020919628

Trafford rev. 10/07/2020

www.trafford.com
North America & international
toll-free: 844-688-6899 (USA & Canada)
fax: 812 355 4082

A special *thank you* to the partners that contributed to the publishing of this book.

Luther and Betty Raines

Ronnie Raines

Quinard and Erlene Shelnutt

Ken and Sherrie Kagey

Esther Medina

Gracie Sutherland

Cathy Nelson

B&S Farm

Barry and Joyce Dalton

INTRODUCTION

Modern Disciples 365 was written by Kevin Raines to motivate believers to not wax cold in their belief as a Christian and to encourage their Christian walk with a word that will bring an impact to pursue a deeper level of commitment toward sincere Godly discipleship.

Here are 365 daily motivational quotes that will empower and give fresh perspective with relevant word. There is truth and freedom throughout God's Holy Word. All quotes in the *Modern Disciples 365* are inspired by the Living Word of God.

God is calling a generation of believers to stand in these last days and be committed in their faith.

ABOUT THE AUTHOR

Kevin Raines delivers a powerful message through diverse platforms of creativity, generating innovative concepts in ministry, design, and production. His unique style of delivery and dedication in reaching others has proven fruitful in multicultural communities and ministry outreaches. He is the lead pastor for Encounter Ministries Inc. Kevin's latest creation is the Modern Disciples brand—a brand created to empower a strong faith movement in modern times. It's become common to be labeled a modern Christian, but a true follower of Jesus Christ, with sincere devotion, will go beyond the label of Christian and rise to the call of Modern Disciples.

WHY DO WE NEED MODERN DISCIPLES TODAY AND NOT JUST MODERN CHRISTIANS?

Modern: Relating to the present as opposed to the remote past. (The past only needs to be reflected, not relived. Stay *relevant*. Stay *modern*.)

Christian: *Christian* usually refers to the following:

- People who follow or adhere to Christianity
- Anything pertaining to Christianity (Wilkipedia)

Modern Christianity has become so widely portrayed as a status position in society instead of a statement of one's profession in true faith.

Disciple: In Christianity, *disciple* primarily refers to a dedicated follower of Jesus (Wikipedia).

Modern Christian: An individual who has awareness and acceptance of Jesus Christ. One who has learned to know of **Him**.

Modern disciple: An individual who follows Jesus Christ and **His** teachings. One who has learned to obey and follow after **Him**.

(Matthew 7:23)

Born to be . . . ?

Only your pursuit can
make it complete.

Reflection: _____

_____

_____

_____

_____

_____

1

Your Godgiven purpose
will always be defined
by your difference.

Reflection: _____

_____

_____

_____

_____

_____

We no longer view vision
with promise, but simply
scale it to popularity.

Reflection: _____

_____

_____

_____

_____

_____

Why is church optional
for so many?

Because *truth* is now only
viewed as optional opinions.

Reflection: _____

_____

_____

_____

_____

_____

You lose your way by finding
comfort in the wilderness.

Reflection: _____

_____

_____

_____

_____

_____

Purposed pain will promote the process to greater position.

Reflection: _____

_____

_____

_____

_____

_____

Sharing your faith can keep
someone from eternally dying.
Sharing your love can keep
someone eternally living.

Reflection: _____

_____

_____

_____

_____

_____

Religious people point
out the don'ts.

Disciples define the dos.

Reflection: _____
_____
_____
_____
_____
_____

The enemy uses the intensity
of the temptation to divert us
from pursuing the course.

Reflection: _____

_____

_____

_____

_____

_____

Distractions are one of man's greatest weaknesses.

Reflection: _____

_____

_____

_____

_____

_____

Something worse than a
no is never even asking!

Reflection: _____

_____

_____

_____

_____

_____

You have to practice the
plan of God before you can
fully perform with purpose.

Reflection: _____
_____
_____
_____
_____
_____

Success:

1. Commit to purpose

2. Commit to endure

3. Commit to complete

4. Commit to repeat

Reflection: _____

_____

_____

_____

_____

_____

_____

Love with your life.

Give with your *all*.

Reflection: _____

_____

_____

_____

_____

_____

That which you dwell
on, you will dwell in.

Reflection: _____

_____

_____

_____

_____

_____

If you put your focus in the direction of darkness, you will end up going there.

Reflection: _____

_____

_____

_____

_____

_____

The reason for life lessons
are not to learn facts but
to never forget truths.

Reflection: _____

_____

_____

_____

_____

_____

Remember the reason
why some ministers are not
fruitful: You can't bribe God's
anointing like you do people.

Reflection: _____
_____
_____
_____
_____
_____

Fear is of the dark world
that decreases vision.

Reflection: _____

_____

_____

_____

_____

_____

The prodigal son mentality:

You may accept the benefits from your Father, but you have underestimated **His** provision."

Reflection: _____

_____

_____

_____

_____

_____

Jesus never randomly gave
out miracles; they were always
manifested through faith.

Reflection: _____

_____

_____

_____

_____

_____

We are robbed so many
times from a blessed
life by the covenant we
made with the enemy.

Reflection: _____

_____

_____

_____

_____

_____

Fear is conceived by an
unprotected mindset called
lack of knowledge.

Reflection: _____

_____

_____

_____

_____

_____

A disobedient response might create a temporary fix, but it will reject a lifetime fulfillment.

Reflection: _____

_____

_____

_____

_____

_____

There is a liberation in learning labels are limitations.

Reflection: _____

_____

_____

_____

_____

_____

Relationship with God requires reading what **He** wrote to you (*Bible*).

Reflection: _____

_____

_____

_____

_____

_____

Your persistence to resist
your own way provokes a
greater God-presence.

Reflection: _____

_____

_____

_____

_____

_____

Faith cannot tell time.

Reflection: _____

_____

_____

_____

_____

_____

Mary, Jesus's mother, was willing to take on shame to fulfill her call.

Reflection: _____

_____

_____

_____

_____

_____

Saying yes to God may
not be popular.

Reflection: _____

_____

_____

_____

_____

_____

Favor is for service, not status.

Reflection: _____

_____

_____

_____

_____

_____

It's not what you can't do; it's what **He** can do through you.

Reflection: _____

_____

_____

_____

_____

_____

He has been known to interrupt our designed plans for **His** divine purpose.

Reflection: _____

_____

_____

_____

_____

_____

We disqualify God by saying it's impossible.

Reflection: _____

_____

_____

_____

_____

_____

If God knows the outcome, then my greatest commitment is trust.

Reflection: _____
_____
_____
_____
_____
_____

Does your will to make a
difference exceed your enemy's
will to destroy your difference?

Reflection: _____
_____
_____
_____
_____
_____

If it damages you in the process,
it shouldn't be called successful.

Reflection: _____

_____

_____

_____

_____

_____

God's greatest disappointment
is when we no longer showcase
the need of **His** existence.

Reflection: _____

_____

_____

_____

_____

_____

A true servant searches
for what they can give not
what they can receive.

Reflection: _____

_____

_____

_____

_____

_____

I'd rather possess the principles of purpose instead of the power of popularity.

Reflection: _____
_____
_____
_____
_____
_____

Never underestimate your how long, but be ready every moment for your when.

Reflection: _____

_____

_____

_____

_____

_____

What if it takes a lifetime of preparation for a time of your life moment, would you still purse?

Reflection: _____

_____

_____

_____

_____

_____

Salvation is not just your access into heaven; it's about Christ's access into you.

Reflection: _____

_____

_____

_____

_____

_____

Your resistance to believe the devil's lie comes by walking out what has not yet been seen.

Reflection: _____

_____

_____

_____

_____

_____

Your faith is what destroys
your adversary.

Reflection: _____

_____

_____

_____

_____

_____

When your worship turns
traditional your encounter
will be unspiritual.

Reflection: _____

_____

_____

_____

_____

_____

Tradition can't completely fuel expectation.

Reflection: _____

_____

_____

_____

_____

_____

Becoming who I am created
to be, not what circumstances
are predicting over me.

Reflection: _____

_____

_____

_____

_____

_____

A great leader learned to follow greatly.

Reflection: _____

_____

_____

_____

_____

_____

Change must occur to equip you for the next season.

Reflection: _____
_____
_____
_____
_____
_____

Change starts with perception
then is defined by direction.

Reflection: _____

_____

_____

_____

_____

_____

God has given you a
promise, not a prediction.

Reflection: _____

_____

_____

_____

_____

_____

Resist trouble, raise peace.

Stand for change, not chaos.

Reflection: _____

_____

_____

_____

_____

_____

Opinions are useless if motives are abusive.

Reflection: _____

_____

_____

_____

_____

_____

Being in the right season
can increase your harvest.
Being in the right time
can increase your life.

Reflection: _____

_____

_____

_____

_____

_____

Expectation is preparation
for impartation.

Don't forfeit the finish.

Reflection: _____

_____

_____

_____

_____

_____

Ignorance responds with harsh words; wisdom responds with a soft answer.

Reflection: _____

_____

_____

_____

_____

_____

Distractions can be deadly to a dream!

Reflection: _____

_____

_____

_____

_____

_____

What distractions minimize your breakthrough?

Reflection: _____

_____

_____

_____

_____

_____

His voice can be discerned in the quest to pursue **His** Word.

Reflection: _____

_____

_____

_____

_____

_____

Don't tarnish God's Word with anxious phrases.

Reflection: _____

_____

_____

_____

_____

_____

_____

You are more than what the
mirror interprets today!

Reflection: _____

_____

_____

_____

_____

_____

You can't take good advise
in an anxious mindset.

Reflection: _____

_____

_____

_____

_____

_____

_____

You can't entertain an
I'm-gonna-fix-it attitude
and stand in faith too.

Reflection: _____

_____

_____

_____

_____

_____

The danger with religion is mixing personal convictions with biblical truths.

Reflection: _____
_____
_____
_____
_____
_____
_____

"Some people say they can't paint a picture because they don't have the right paint . . . It's not about the paint, it's about the passion" (Gina Raines).

Reflection: _____

_____

_____

_____

_____

_____

Knowledge is knowing the difference between the Gospel and demonic gossip.

Reflection: _____

_____

_____

_____

_____

_____

My lack could be a simple learning tool to create in me the potential to be a better provider.

Reflection: _____

_____

_____

_____

_____

_____

God doesn't promise provision to petty pretenders; **He** promises provision to practicing providers of purpose.

Reflection: _____

_____

_____

_____

_____

_____

_____

The follow-through is greater
than the want to.

Reflection: _____

_____

_____

_____

_____

_____

You might be willing, but are you obedient?

Reflection: _____

_____

_____

_____

_____

_____

_____

Thank God, I was only given
enough to destroy my desire
and not my destiny.

Reflection: _____

_____

_____

_____

_____

_____

A fake smile might pacify, but a genuine smile will gratify.

Reflection: _____

_____

_____

_____

_____

_____

God doesn't just know the outcome; **He** *is* the outcome.

Reflection: _____

_____

_____

_____

_____

_____

The mindset to settle is extremely dangerous to your destiny.

Reflection: _____

_____

_____

_____

_____

_____

May your outcome be more
about what you overcome
than what overwhelms.

Reflection: _____

_____

_____

_____

_____

_____

A real leader is willing to lose
the comfort of position to lead
in a place of discomfort.

Reflection: _____

_____

_____

_____

_____

_____

Sometimes the greatest
display of strength is
revealed through humility.

Reflection: _____

_____

_____

_____

_____

_____

If you can't be truthful, then you can't be real.

Reflection: _____

_____

_____

_____

_____

_____

Don't get caught up looking at
what they have and lose sight of
what you own. Envy is an enemy.

Reflection: _____

_____

_____

_____

_____

_____

If you want to perform with purpose, then practice direction.

Reflection: _____

_____

_____

_____

_____

_____

You can't be successful if we are not willing to see others succeed.

Reflection: _____

_____

_____

_____

_____

_____

What have you been
underestimating that
God is ready to use?

Reflection: _____

_____

_____

_____

_____

_____

_____

Keep looking—the miracle
could be in the madness.

Reflection: _____

_____

_____

_____

_____

_____

Your potential is poised
in your pursuit.

Reflection: _____
_____
_____
_____
_____
_____

Passive will never be able to have a real conversation with progress.

Reflection: _____
_____
_____
_____
_____
_____
_____

Sneaky will never satisfy stability!

Reflection: _____

_____

_____

_____

_____

_____

_____

Where are you in your next step?

Starting, leaving, complaining, or completing?

Reflection: _____

_____

_____

_____

_____

_____

Avoidance creates a larger void.

Reflection: _____

_____

_____

_____

_____

_____

It's not the voices you hear that make a difference; it's the one you choose to follow.

Reflection: _____

_____

_____

_____

_____

_____

You can't solve a problem in the same mindset it was created in.

Reflection: _____

_____

_____

_____

_____

_____

God will never take you back
to a place that smothered
your fire without first
starting a greater blaze.

Reflection: _____

_____

_____

_____

_____

_____

The best motivation can be obtained from the worst of days.

Reflection: _____

_____

_____

_____

_____

_____

Your talent isn't what impresses
God; your obedience
through faith does.

Reflection: _____
_____
_____
_____
_____
_____

Your calling doesn't gain access to **His** glory, your response to **His** instruction does.

Reflection: _____

_____

_____

_____

_____

_____

Your promise might be
packaged slightly different
than your perspective.

Reflection: _____

_____

_____

_____

_____

_____

Never belittle beginning small.

Reflection: _____

_____

_____

_____

_____

_____

If we used our gifts more unselfishly, we would see the world more gratefully.

Reflection: _____

_____

_____

_____

_____

_____

It might become troubling and trying, but greater is the promise to triumph.

Reflection: _____

_____

_____

_____

_____

_____

Restrictions can reap rewards
even if the opportunity is
pursued in confinement.

Reflection: _____
_____
_____
_____
_____
_____

Isolated times can be the best confirmation that God needs your full attention.

Reflection: _____

_____

_____

_____

_____

_____

_____

Some will suggest a restart and revision, while others will long for restoration and revival. Those shall be called the remnant.

Reflection: _____

_____

_____

_____

_____

_____

It takes more effort to look the part . . . For once, just be it.

Reflection: _____

_____

_____

_____

_____

_____

In the end, some will realize that the very thing that was taken for granted is now seen as a strong need.

Reflection: _____

_____

_____

_____

_____

_____

The promise will take determination.

The process will take dedication.

The promise will come when the process is pursued!

Reflection: _____

_____

_____

_____

_____

_____

You will never receive complete
victory until you confront the
fear that hides you from it.

Reflection: _____

_____

_____

_____

_____

_____

It's not how many members come through the doors of a church; it's how many disciples that can be sent out of them.

Reflection: _____

_____

_____

_____

_____

_____

_____

If you have an excuse for every challenging thing you do, then discovering purpose will be one of the most impossible things you will do.

Reflection: _____

_____

_____

_____

_____

_____

The disruptions just might be part of your destiny.

Reflection: _____

_____

_____

_____

_____

_____

Don't ruin today by worrying about tomorrow.

Reflection: _____
_____
_____
_____
_____
_____

I will be inspired by my
trial, not intimidated.

Reflection: _____
_____
_____
_____
_____
_____
_____

Fear is strikingly terrifying, but
faith is terrifyingly striking.

Reflection: _____

_____

_____

_____

_____

_____

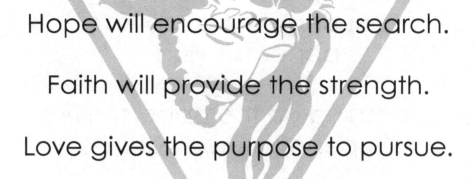

Hope will encourage the search.

Faith will provide the strength.

Love gives the purpose to pursue.

Reflection: _____

_____

_____

_____

_____

_____

Focusing on the problem
perfects failure.

Focusing on the opportunity
perfects precision.

Reflection: _____

_____

_____

_____

_____

_____

Is your faith being affected or
infected by today's opportunity?

Reflection: _____

_____

_____

_____

_____

_____

If you just put on the armor of God the way you put on hand sanitizer, imagine the impact.

Reflection: _____

_____

_____

_____

_____

_____

Divine opportunities
can come disguised as
devastating problems. Keep
pursuing the opportunity.

Reflection: _____

_____

_____

_____

_____

_____

Your discussions will dictate your destiny.

Reflection: _____

_____

_____

_____

_____

_____

It's time to make the church powerful, not popular.

Reflection: _____

_____

_____

_____

_____

_____

Don't let your dream kill your God-moment.

Reflection: _____
_____
_____
_____
_____
_____

Often, the most valuable
gifts will come through
the suffering of loss.

Reflection: _____

_____

_____

_____

_____

_____

Are you looking desperate or destined?

Reflection: _____

_____

_____

_____

_____

_____

Darkness has never been a defeating fear factor for God.

Reflection: _____

_____

_____

_____

_____

_____

Remember, the one that
wanted the role of God no
longer lives with God.

Reflection: _____

_____

_____

_____

_____

_____

Judging someone's praise
will leave you barren—just
ask King David's wife!

Reflection: _____
_____
_____
_____
_____
_____

You can't be blessed if you're convincing your conviction to play another role other than obedience.

Reflection: _____
_____
_____
_____
_____
_____

Make today as beautiful as the brilliance of a morning sunrise.

Reflection: _____

_____

_____

_____

_____

_____

Be willing to water your faith with God's Word instead of watering down your faith with worry.

Reflection: _____

_____

_____

_____

_____

_____

You have not because you
ask not; you receive not
because you believe not.

Reflection: _____
_____
_____
_____
_____
_____
_____

Your miracle can be motivated
only by your movement.

Reflection: _____
_____
_____
_____
_____
_____

Don't judge someone's journey just because it looks different than yours . . .
That's called ignorance.

Reflection: _____

_____

_____

_____

_____

_____

Every mastered instruction
creates an access to increase.

Reflection: _____

_____

_____

_____

_____

_____

Don't just view yourself in a position; view it as placed purpose!

Reflection: _____

_____

_____

_____

_____

_____

"If faith the size of a mustard seed can move mountains, what could faith the size of a mountain move?" (Kolten Raines)

Reflection: _____

_____

_____

_____

_____

_____

Don't get so caught up in
the style of worship that you
forget the sacredness of it.

Reflection: _____

_____

_____

_____

_____

_____

God's not looking for
perfection, just persistence!

Reflection: _____

_____

_____

_____

_____

_____

When fear has a right to speak, but faith silences it!

Reflection: _____

_____

_____

_____

_____

_____

Purpose isn't always pretty,
but it is always powerful.

Reflection: _____

_____

_____

_____

_____

_____

Your greatest qualities
can be produced through
your greatest failures.

Reflection: _____
_____
_____
_____
_____
_____

You can't curse what you won't confront.

Reflection: _____
_____
_____
_____
_____
_____

You can't think like a donkey
and fly like an eagle.

Reflection: _____

_____

_____

_____

_____

_____

Opposition is an opportunity to clearly define your objectives.

Reflection: _____

_____

_____

_____

_____

_____

Resets are required
to reach goals.

Reflection: _____

_____

_____

_____

_____

_____

It's hard knowing real joy if
you don't first witness pain.

Reflection: _____

_____

_____

_____

_____

_____

Opposition is an opportunity
to showcase that much
more optimism.

Reflection: _____

_____

_____

_____

_____

_____

Don't strive to be famous, strive to be influential.

Reflection: _____

_____

_____

_____

_____

_____

Opportunities are a
pursuant's dream.

Opportunities are a
procrastinator's nightmare.

One sees a blessing; the
other sees a curse.

Reflection: _____

_____

_____

_____

_____

_____

Legends fight for purpose,
not popularity.

Reflection: _____

_____

_____

_____

_____

_____

Progression is a visual stimulant
to your process, which brings
awareness that your course
is still worth pursuing.

Reflection: _____

_____

_____

_____

_____

_____

Projecting vision is called faith.

Projecting failure is called fear.

What you project is vital.

Reflection: _____

_____

_____

_____

_____

_____

If you want to become the couture of destiny, start something and pursue it with purpose and passion.

Reflection: _____

_____

_____

_____

_____

_____

Specifics to purpose is your communication with destiny.

Reflection: _____

_____

_____

_____

_____

_____

It's not happy moments
that set dreams in motion;
it's habit moments.

Reflection: _____

_____

_____

_____

_____

_____

Opportunists seek opportunities, not excuses.

Reflection: _____

_____

_____

_____

_____

_____

See! It took pain and prayer to pull out purpose. Running from either could create purpose failure.

Reflection: _____

_____

_____

_____

_____

_____

We should want our churches full
of conversions, not members!

Reflection: _____

_____

_____

_____

_____

_____

Even if you feel you are getting
nowhere, the fact remains
you are still somewhere.

Reflection: _____

_____

_____

_____

_____

_____

Don't let pretending be
part of your purpose.

Reflection: _____

_____

_____

_____

_____

_____

I'm called driven, not just career driven.

Reflection: _____

_____

_____

_____

_____

_____

Discipline is a very hard habit to create, but a very effective one.

Reflection: _____

_____

_____

_____

_____

_____

Pharisees describe the don'ts.

Disciples define the dos.

Reflection: _____

_____

_____

_____

_____

_____

_____

Your preservation may be your
protection until your promise
comes into positioned.

Reflection: _____

_____

_____

_____

_____

_____

I'd rather be mixed-up color
than remain a blank canvas.

Reflection: _____

_____

_____

_____

_____

_____

Your calling is much higher than simply running away.

Reflection: _____

_____

_____

_____

_____

_____

Moments from your past, whether failures or successes, can be used to create character that will be very beneficial for your present.

Reflection: _____

_____

_____

_____

_____

_____

I want God to move in
places money can't buy.

Reflection: _____
_____
_____
_____
_____
_____

You are never too young
to start purpose.

You are never too old
to stop purpose.

Reflection: _____

_____

_____

_____

_____

_____

Your past battles prepared
you for present purpose.

Reflection: _____

_____

_____

_____

_____

_____

When expectation turns to excuses, dreams are delayed.

Reflection: _____

_____

_____

_____

_____

_____

_____

Everything that ever became successful never started simple.

Reflection: _____
_____
_____
_____
_____
_____

Details are vital when
opportunity is present.

Reflection: _____

_____

_____

_____

_____

_____

Choose to be original today!

Reflection: _____

_____

_____

_____

_____

_____

You are worth saving.

Your value never
decreases with God.

Reflection: _____

_____

_____

_____

_____

_____

_____

The adversary will remind
you that you are used and
abused and not worth it, but
be reminded every morning,
God says you can be new.

Reflection: _____

_____

_____

_____

_____

_____

Build for the battle,

Build from the bottom,

Build with a God brilliance,

Build with boldness—

Just keep building!

Reflection: _____

_____

_____

_____

_____

_____

It wouldn't be intimidating
if you weren't building
something bigger than you!

Reflection: _____

_____

_____

_____

_____

_____

A promise from God is expectation exposed through reality.

Reflection: _____

_____

_____

_____

_____

_____

Don't let the prison place
manipulate you into doubt.

Reflection: _____
_____
_____
_____
_____
_____

Your identity determines your view of purpose. If you are in a loss of identity, then you will be lost without purpose.

Reflection: _____

_____

_____

_____

_____

_____

Premature blessings will
birth mature problems.

Reflection: _____
_____
_____
_____
_____
_____

Complacent living exiles
kingdom access.

Reflection: _____

_____

_____

_____

_____

_____

Are you building for the
purpose of **His** kingdom, or
has your kingdom become
your soul purpose?

Reflection: _____
_____
_____
_____
_____
_____

Do you put more focus on who you *want* to be or who you were created to be?

Reflection: _____

_____

_____

_____

_____

_____

We try comparing our canoe
to someone's ship, but never
consider the cost that was
invested to construct it.

Reflection: _____
_____
_____
_____
_____
_____

Petty drama develops
when people try masking
who they really are.

Reflection: _____

_____

_____

_____

_____

_____

We loose faith because we have disconnected from hope, which causes our expectation to cease.

Reflection: _____

_____

_____

_____

_____

_____

Labels define people to categories that were created by the judgments of men.

Reflection: _____

_____

_____

_____

_____

_____

_____

Don't doom your destiny with negative words.

Reflection: _____

_____

_____

_____

_____

_____

Real *faith* must go beyond basic belief and begin with action.

Reflection: _____

_____

_____

_____

_____

_____

Your devotion to God creates
the need for **Him** to still
be priority in your life.

Reflection: _____

_____

_____

_____

_____

_____

Real devotion to God brings
out the real character of God.

Reflection: _____

_____

_____

_____

_____

_____

The intensity of the fight will
reveal the contents of the war.

Reflection: _____

_____

_____

_____

_____

_____

Form habits that are long lasting, not momentary.

Reflection: _____

_____

_____

_____

_____

_____

Don't do it to impress; do it to create impact.

Reflection: _____

_____

_____

_____

_____

_____

Godly transitions are always
designed for promotion.

Reflection: _____

_____

_____

_____

_____

_____

If you have to hide it, then it's probably called ungodly.

Reflection: _____

_____

_____

_____

_____

_____

Confusion is designed to create dysfunction.

Reflection: _____

_____

_____

_____

_____

_____

You can encounter disastrous
moments but still dwell
in perfect peace.

Reflection: _____

_____

_____

_____

_____

_____

Unity is truly a God-created portion of life that is breathtakingly amazing!

Reflection: _____

_____

_____

_____

_____

_____

You can have lack and luxury in the same view, but what you choose to see becomes your perspective.

Reflection: _____

_____

_____

_____

_____

_____

God's invitations just might be
hidden in **His** instructions.

Reflection: _____

_____

_____

_____

_____

_____

Am I following through what God has already approved?

Reflection: _____

_____

_____

_____

_____

_____

What if we chased God as persistent as we chased our worldly obsession?

Reflection: _____

_____

_____

_____

_____

_____

What if I gave God as much
of my mind as I give to
anxiety, doubt, and lust?

Reflection: _____

_____

_____

_____

_____

_____

No lack isn't the total sum of materialistic gains; no lack is the sum of my need provided in **His** name.

Reflection: _____

_____

_____

_____

_____

_____

I'd rather go through hell
in this life than to live in
it in the next one.

Reflection: _____

_____

_____

_____

_____

_____

Your harvest is about to change because of the knowledge you've obtained.

Reflection: _____
_____
_____
_____
_____
_____

Your *no* might very well be an open door to destiny.

Reflection: _____

_____

_____

_____

_____

_____

Your denial might be another's access to deliverance.

Reflection: _____

_____

_____

_____

_____

_____

_____

Don't get frustrated in your failed attempts; it was still fruitful because you are still willing to pursue.

Reflection: _____

_____

_____

_____

_____

_____

Put the same efforts in preparing
for the temporary as you
do for the permanent.

It's called the product of integrity.

Reflection: _____

_____

_____

_____

_____

_____

Your persistence is what
produces the prize.

Reflection: _____
_____
_____
_____
_____
_____

The process allows you to reflect on where you've been and embrace where you are still going.

Reflection: _____

_____

_____

_____

_____

_____

The enemy uses the intensity
of the temptation to divert
us from the course.

Reflection: _____

_____

_____

_____

_____

_____

The enemy wants us to spend a lifetime trying to discover what we are. Meanwhile, God has destined us to discover who we are.

Reflection: _____

_____

_____

_____

_____

_____

Don't let your treasure
become your trap.

Reflection: _____

_____

_____

_____

_____

_____

Don't let your obligation to God override your obedience to **Him.**

Reflection: _____

_____

_____

_____

_____

_____

The solution to the problem might be in the sum of: are you stuck on the question or the answer?

Reflection: _____

_____

_____

_____

_____

_____

Continue to trust God fully. A relocation could be a promise land and not a settlement.

Reflection: _____

_____

_____

_____

_____

_____

Don't work to be seen;
work to fulfill the dream.

Reflection: _____

_____

_____

_____

_____

_____

Your labor is a blessing from God.

It's a way to honor **Him**
in everyday life.

Reflection: _____

_____

_____

_____

_____

_____

Your job is an opportunity to serve and witness to people throughout the day. Be vigilant!

Reflection: _____

_____

_____

_____

_____

_____

Religious people pay more attention in deciphering shoe styles verses discerning spirits.

Reflection: _____

_____

_____

_____

_____

_____

Just because God fights for you doesn't mean you should be absent from the fight.

Reflection: _____

_____

_____

_____

_____

_____

Persistence in your faith,
prayer, and worship make
all the difference.

Reflection: _____

_____

_____

_____

_____

_____

Your faith can produce change today in the midst of crazy circumstances.

Reflection: _____

_____

_____

_____

_____

_____

Don't just live by the testimony
of yesterday, live out the
testimony of today.

Reflection: _____
_____
_____
_____
_____
_____

Fear is conceived upon lack of knowledge.

Reflection: _____

_____

_____

_____

_____

_____

Expectation creates an
environment for successful
opportunities.

Reflection: _____

_____

_____

_____

_____

_____

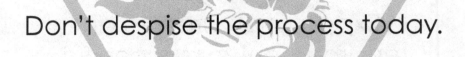

Don't despise the process today.

Reflection: _____

_____

_____

_____

_____

_____

Don't let time restrictions damper your expectations.

Reflection: _____

_____

_____

_____

_____

_____

_____

The greater miracle is what
develops inside of you
through the process.

Reflection: _____

_____

_____

_____

_____

_____

Heaven and hell both have conversations about you. What you chose to listen to determines which one becomes your truth.

Reflection: _____

_____

_____

_____

_____

_____

Remember, self-sufficiency cripples the movement of God.

Reflection: _____

_____

_____

_____

_____

_____

Your greatest victory is hidden
in your greatest finish.

Reflection: _____

_____

_____

_____

_____

_____

What looks like a hindrance
today could be your
help tomorrow.

Reflection: _____

_____

_____

_____

_____

_____

When victories succeed,
opportunities increase.

Reflection: _____

_____

_____

_____

_____

_____

Don't let the unknown
be a seed to fear.

Reflection: _____
_____
_____
_____
_____
_____

Satan is the organizer
of breakdown.

God is the organizer
of breakthrough.

What are you allowing to
be organized within you?

Reflection: _____

_____

_____

_____

_____

_____

My level of worship to God will determined my position of reception.

Reflection: _____

_____

_____

_____

_____

_____

Your difference doesn't just define you, it completely sets you apart.

Reflection: _____

_____

_____

_____

_____

_____

_____

Do something wrong for a period of time, you will find insanity.

Do something right for a period of time, you will find success.

Reflection: _____

_____

_____

_____

_____

_____

Determination is the power
that forces success in your life.

Reflection: _____

_____

_____

_____

_____

_____

Your choices today become
your living tomorrow.

Reflection: _____
_____
_____
_____
_____
_____

Obstacles become the
motivation that highlights
the clearer path.

Reflection: _____
_____
_____
_____
_____
_____

Failure will be poking when favor starts peeking.

Reflection: _____

_____

_____

_____

_____

_____

Persecution will always appear before promotion.

Reflection: _____

_____

_____

_____

_____

_____

One must become truly grateful
before they can be greatly used.

Reflection: _____

_____

_____

_____

_____

_____

Confronting devils isn't comfortable, but it's necessary.

Reflection: _____

_____

_____

_____

_____

_____

_____

It's more than being right;
it's about being light.

Reflection: _____

_____

_____

_____

_____

_____

Some checks facts, I
choose to check acts.

(Actions truly do speak
louder than words.)

Reflection: _____

_____

_____

_____

_____

_____

A sinner might die rich, but a Christian dies obtaining riches.

Reflection: _____

_____

_____

_____

_____

_____

God brings provision through acts of obedience.

(Note: Provision isn't always money.)

Reflection: _____

_____

_____

_____

_____

_____

A leader's best ability isn't how well they can handle acceptance; it's how well they can handle rejection.

Reflection: _____

_____

_____

_____

_____

_____

Prophesy requires position
and preparation to fulfillment.
You are required to walk
out what was spoken.

Reflection: _____

_____

_____

_____

_____

_____

Jesus is coming back for an interracial bride—all races taking one place!

Reflection: _____

_____

_____

_____

_____

_____

Balance is a belief that
births blessings.

Reflection: _____

_____

_____

_____

_____

_____

You only really need *one* reason to worship God: **Him**.

Reflection: _____

_____

_____

_____

_____

_____

It takes more than a desire
to see a move of God; it will
require true conviction.

Reflection: _____

_____

_____

_____

_____

_____

Check yourself—self-righteousness isn't a fruit of the Spirit.

Reflection: _____
_____
_____
_____
_____
_____

Sometimes you just have
to say *it's enough!*

Reflection: _____

_____

_____

_____

_____

_____

Don't let desensitization
be an excuse to not work
for God's kingdom.

Reflection: _____

_____

_____

_____

_____

_____

Your level of wisdom can only exceed to the level of experiences you encounter.

Reflection: _____

_____

_____

_____

_____

_____

Vision is vital for victory.

Reflection: _____

_____

_____

_____

_____

_____

If your imagery is distorted, then
your vision will be impaired.

Reflection: _____

_____

_____

_____

_____

_____

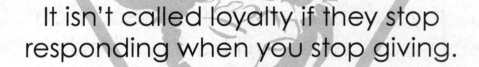

It isn't called loyalty if they stop responding when you stop giving.

Reflection: _____

_____

_____

_____

_____

_____

The full follow-through is
what many never do.

Reflection: _____

_____

_____

_____

_____

_____

_____

Comfort will increase compromise.

Reflection: _____

_____

_____

_____

_____

_____

You aren't called to compromise;
you are called to commit.

Reflection: _____

_____

_____

_____

_____

_____

_____

We should need to . . . not just
want to or even have to.

Reflection: _____

_____

_____

_____

_____

_____

_____

The level of your influence
will be revealed through
the level of your impact.

Reflection: _____

_____

_____

_____

_____

_____

Procrastination never plays
well with purpose.

Reflection: _____

_____

_____

_____

_____

_____

Don't let the words you say
and the actions you live have
two different conversations.

Reflection: _____

_____

_____

_____

_____

_____

_____

Don't let your issues affect what you commit to. Step it up!

Reflection: _____

_____

_____

_____

_____

_____

There is *no* excuse too intellectual to justify why purpose can't be pursued.

Reflection: _____

_____

_____

_____

_____

_____

Stop calling for justice to try
and justify the consequences
of dumb decisions!

Reflection: _____

_____

_____

_____

_____

_____

You can doom your destiny
by the words you say and
the actions that follows.

Reflection: _____

_____

_____

_____

_____

_____

Desire misdirected can cause vision loss.

Reflection: _____

_____

_____

_____

_____

_____

Recognize the bait of
your weakness; it's rooted
in your desires.

Reflection: _____

_____

_____

_____

_____

_____

It wasn't how successful Peter could walk on water; the key was keeping his eye on Jesus.

Reflection: _____

_____

_____

_____

_____

_____

Your words and freewill
decide the conversation
God speaks over your life.

Reflection: _____

_____

_____

_____

_____

_____

_____

Your greatest struggles will produce your greatest blessings.

Reflection: _____

_____

_____

_____

_____

_____

He will finish what **He** started if you will start what **He** is finishing.

Reflection: _____

_____

_____

_____

_____

_____

You can never fully
understand what you've
never truly encountered.

Reflection: _____
_____
_____
_____
_____
_____

Some people will never get past your past to see your full potential.

Reflection: _____

_____

_____

_____

_____

_____

_____

You have to commit to instruction
before starting production.

Reflection: _____

_____

_____

_____

_____

_____

Don't be so successful you
can't lose the grip of pride.

Reflection: _____

_____

_____

_____

_____

_____

289

Don't ever get too big
to admit a defeat.

Reflection: _____

_____

_____

_____

_____

_____

Some people might be
used in your pain to pull
out your best potential.

Reflection: _____
_____
_____
_____
_____
_____

Some people will respect your presence, but not your position.

Reflection: _____

_____

_____

_____

_____

_____

Don't become so comfortable
that you can't make changes
for what's coming.

Reflection: _____

_____

_____

_____

_____

_____

Some battles you face
are to build character,
not to beat you down.

Reflection: _____
_____
_____
_____
_____
_____

Sometimes it's the words you
don't say in front of others that
establish wisdom in your life.

Reflection: _____

_____

_____

_____

_____

_____

Battles you conquer
inwardly will bring about a
deeper kingdom praise.

Reflection: _____

_____

_____

_____

_____

_____

Sometimes it is more than just conquering the individual, it's about establishing the next God position in your life.

Reflection: _____

_____

_____

_____

_____

_____

Don't become so positioned you can no longer seek direction.

Reflection: _____

_____

_____

_____

_____

_____

Even though you have the advantage to win, God may want to use that person for more than one season in your life.

Reflection: _____

_____

_____

_____

_____

_____

Moments of isolation in
complete adoration will
reveal the heart of God.

Reflection: _____

_____

_____

_____

_____

_____

It's more than just winning a battle of war; its truly knowing what you are fighting for.

Reflection: _____

_____

_____

_____

_____

_____

Warriors are weaker when they
are caught without a weapon.

Reflection: _____

_____

_____

_____

_____

_____

Warriors without worship
are immature.

Reflection: _____

_____

_____

_____

_____

_____

Don't begin a new battle
with a new weapon.

Reflection: _____
_____
_____
_____
_____
_____

Accessing any new thing will require accountable action.

Reflection: _____

_____

_____

_____

_____

_____

Sometimes you just have to do what you don't feel like doing.

Reflection: _____

_____

_____

_____

_____

_____

In order for destiny to be directed, you might have to play a role outside your comfort zone.

Reflection: _____

_____

_____

_____

_____

_____

Don't be fooled by a desperate person's words.

Reflection: _____

_____

_____

_____

_____

_____

Remember, breakthrough
is fear's biggest critic.

Reflection: _____

_____

_____

_____

_____

_____

Joy is depression's greatest rival.

Reflection: _____

_____

_____

_____

_____

_____

Praise is pain's worst nightmare.

Reflection: _____

_____

_____

_____

_____

_____

God confidence is intimidation's toughest hit.

Reflection: _____

_____

_____

_____

_____

_____

Hope is faith's best weapon.

Reflection: _____

_____

_____

_____

_____

_____

Don't expect your purpose to fit in certain places.

Reflection: _____

_____

_____

_____

_____

_____

Adversity will bring you into a place of distraction if you let it.

Reflection: _____

_____

_____

_____

_____

_____

_____

You are becoming something
right now, whether you
realize it or not.

Reflection: _____

_____

_____

_____

_____

_____

_____

Your decisions are the
driver of your destiny.

Reflection: _____

_____

_____

_____

_____

_____

Keep your heart humbled,
not hardened.

Reflection: _____

_____

_____

_____

_____

_____

Some places you go with Jesus will require more than a yes, but a true commitment to continue.

Reflection: _____

_____

_____

_____

_____

_____

Don't develop a form of God
and lack the character of **Him**.

Reflection: _____

_____

_____

_____

_____

_____

Could the problem be
defined in what I worship,
not who I worship?

Reflection: _____

_____

_____

_____

_____

_____

The attitude I choose to possess determines the outcome I will receive.

Reflection: _____

_____

_____

_____

_____

_____

Many won't put in the time
it takes to allow greatness to
flow out. Don't be like many.

Reflection: _____

_____

_____

_____

_____

_____

Hope is the raft between
reckless and rescue.

Reflection: _____

_____

_____

_____

_____

_____

Worry can't see past
its present state.

Reflection: _____

_____

_____

_____

_____

_____

It's your choice to end in pieces or in peace.

Reflection: _____

_____

_____

_____

_____

_____

_____

You will thrive when your purpose becomes an obsession.

Reflection: _____

_____

_____

_____

_____

_____

If you can give God your undivided attention, then you will see change for the good.

Reflection: _____

_____

_____

_____

_____

_____

You will never be able to find **Him** if you are never seeking.

Reflection: _____

_____

_____

_____

_____

_____

First step to victory,
identify your enemy!

You wouldn't go after a
lion with a mousetrap.

Reflection: _____

_____

_____

_____

_____

_____

Spiritually speaking, what
you put on in your closet
(prayer closet) determines
your effectiveness in society.

Reflection: _____
_____
_____
_____
_____
_____

You get what you put in.

You receive what you give out.

Reflection: _____
_____
_____
_____
_____
_____

Remember, an altar is
not just for a sinner.

Reflection: _____

_____

_____

_____

_____

_____

You can't have access to certain capabilities unless you invest.

Reflection: _____

_____

_____

_____

_____

_____

Discouragement is a form of
disease contracted by hearing
and believing the wrong
things contrary to promise.

Reflection: _____

_____

_____

_____

_____

_____

How you handle failure will access your level of favor.

Reflection: _____
_____
_____
_____
_____
_____

You can't display courage
unless fear is present.

Reflection: _____

_____

_____

_____

_____

_____

How can God reveal how big **He** is to you if you don't first encounter a crisis?

Reflection: _____

_____

_____

_____

_____

_____

Don't be too busy looking for promotion that you miss purpose.

Reflection: _____

_____

_____

_____

_____

_____

Your enemy's greatest influence
comes through the voice
that feeds your doubt.

Reflection: _____

_____

_____

_____

_____

_____

Your God purpose must be born in you, not borrowed.

Reflection: _____

_____

_____

_____

_____

_____

Your greatest attributes will not be in plain sight; you will have to activate them from within.

Reflection: _____

_____

_____

_____

_____

_____

God stored in you what has been stored in no one else.

Reflection: _____

_____

_____

_____

_____

_____

_____

What are you willing to invest to capture a moment of great success?

Reflection: _____

_____

_____

_____

_____

_____

How long are you willing
to endure to capture one
glimpse of success?

Reflection: _____

_____

_____

_____

_____

_____

Your wait isn't wasteful,
but worth continuing.

Reflection: _____

_____

_____

_____

_____

_____

Sometimes you have to
keep showing up, even
when nothing else does.

Reflection: _____

_____

_____

_____

_____

_____

You can never have too much rehearsal time.

Reflection: _____

_____

_____

_____

_____

_____

Your greatest display of
devotion will be when no
one else is watching.

Reflection: _____

_____

_____

_____

_____

_____

Your trivial motivation is
understanding the value
you bring to the table.

Reflection: _____

_____

_____

_____

_____

_____

No one ever wants to
follow a quitter.

Reflection: _____

_____

_____

_____

_____

_____

Wisdom is not obtained by age; wisdom is obtained by overcoming failure.

Reflection: _____

_____

_____

_____

_____

_____

Your greatest rejection could be God's greatest influence to you.

Reflection: _____

_____

_____

_____

_____

_____

Don't use God's truth to
manipulate your own agenda.

Reflection: _____

_____

_____

_____

_____

_____

The church has done
a fascinating job of
accommodating everyone's
wants, but we've lost what
God requested **He** needs.

Reflection: _____

_____

_____

_____

_____

_____

You first have to make time
before you can make a plan.

Reflection: _____

_____

_____

_____

_____

_____

Removing distractions
activates creativity again.

Reflection: _____

_____

_____

_____

_____

_____

Start viewing every day
as an adventure and
not an avoidance.

Reflection: _____

_____

_____

_____

_____

_____

Great faith disrupts facts.

Reflection: _____

_____

_____

_____

_____

_____

Wisdom simplified =
conquered failure!

Reflection: _____
_____
_____
_____
_____
_____

Your greatest display of devotion to God can be carried out through discipleship.

Reflection: _____

_____

_____

_____

_____

_____